FOURTEEN
Monkeys

A Rain Forest Rhyme

Melissa Stewart
Illustrated by Steve Jenkins

Beach Lane Books   New York London Toronto Sydney New Delhi

Fourteen monkeys share Manú, a warm, lush forest in Peru.

Most tropical rain forests are home to just a few kinds of monkeys. But 14 species live in Manú National Park, in Peru. How can they all survive together in one place?

- They have different body sizes.

- They live at different heights above the ground. ○

- They behave in different ways.

- They eat different foods.

Thanks to these differences, the monkeys don't compete for food or space to live.

Rain forest infographics on each spread include an orange circle that indicates the height in the forest where each monkey lives.

As the sun begins to rise, creatures wake to howler cries.

Each morning, red howler monkeys climb to the tops of the trees and belt out long, loud, bellowing roars. The calls tell other howler groups, "This is our home. Stay away!"

Howlers lead a lazy life. They move slowly and carefully through the trees, searching for tender, tasty leaves. They rest for up to 18 hours a day.

Red howler monkeys

On lengthy legs that stretch with ease,
spider monkeys swing through trees.

Peruvian spider monkeys use their long, limber legs and hook-like feet to glide gracefully through the forest canopy. They move quickly and travel long distances in search of their favorite fruits.

After a morning of feeding, the adults rest and the little ones play. Sometimes moms join in for a game of hide-and-seek or tag.

Peruvian spider monkeys

**Closer to the shady ground,
shaggy sakis leap and bound.**

Gray's bald-faced sakis (SAH-kees) race through the rain forest, using their strong back legs to jump across wide gaps between the trees. Sakis can leap up to 32 feet. Wow!

Many monkeys eat ripe fruit and spit out the seeds. But sakis tear open unripe fruit with their tough teeth and strong jaws. Then they grind and swallow the nutritious seeds.

Gray's bald-faced saki

Capuchins perch with coiled tails,
munching fruit and frogs and snails.

White-fronted capuchin

Brown capuchin

If you see a monkey with a coiled tail, it's probably a capuchin (KAP-yoo-chin). But the two capuchin species at Manú National Park lead very different lives. White-fronted capuchins search for fruit, nuts, and insects high in the forest. Brown capuchins hunt for food closer to or on the ground. Besides fruit and nuts, they'll eat any animal small enough to catch.

Marmosets feed on sugary sap,
then they take a midday nap.

Pygmy marmosets

Pygmy marmosets spend most of the day feeding. They gnaw holes in tree bark and lap up the sweet, sticky sap that oozes out. They also catch grasshoppers, beetles, and other insects.

After a short midday nap, the monkeys pick dirt and dead skin out of one another's fur. Grooming keeps the monkeys clean and healthy. It also builds friendship and trust.

Way up in the leafy crown,
woollys dangle upside down.

Gray woolly monkeys

Gray woolly monkeys move through the treetops at a slow, steady pace. To cross gaps, they hang by their tails and gently lower themselves to the next branch. They also swing by their tails to reach tasty fruit.

These monkeys are friendly and peaceful. They rarely fight, and they greet one another with hugs and kisses.

Goeldi's monkeys spot a snack—

Goeldi's monkeys

chewy fungi in a crack.

Goeldi's (GEL-deez) monkeys spend most of
their time in the forest's dense undergrowth.
They dash along branches and hop across gaps,
landing on all four feet.

    During the wet season, these monkeys eat a
wide variety of foods. But when the rains stop,
they gorge on wrinkly, rubbery fungi that sprout
from cracks in tree bark.

Squirrel monkeys peep and purr,
as they stroke their babies' fur.

Black-capped squirrel monkeys use at least 26 calls to communicate. They twitter to greet one another and bark when they feel threatened. Mama monkeys soothe their babies with gentle peeps and purrs.

These monkeys spend most of their time looking for food. During the heat of midday, they rest and play.

Black-capped squirrel monkeys

When they spot a hungry hawk,
tiny tamarins chirp and squawk.

Emperor tamarin

Tamarins are full of energy. They scurry to the tips of branches to drink nectar and nab insects bigger monkeys can't reach. They also eat fruit and lizards.

As emperor tamarins feed high in the forest, they watch for hawks and harpy eagles. Saddleback tamarins feed closer to the ground. They're always on the lookout for jaguars and ocelots. Traveling together helps both kinds of monkeys stay safe.

Saddleback tamarin

Underneath the bright full moon,
young night monkeys hoot and croon.

What makes black-headed night monkeys so special? They're active after the sun goes down.

On dark nights, these monkeys quietly search for food. But when the moon is bright, families scamper along branches and leap across gaps. Young adults sprint through the forest, hooting loudly for mates. When two monkeys meet, they call to one another, composing a soft, sweet duet.

Black-headed night monkeys

Titis slumber through the night,
with long, thick tails twisted tight.

Dusky titis

Fourteen monkeys share Manú,
a warm, lush forest in Peru.

EMERGENT LAYER

CANOPY

UNDERSTORY

FOREST FLOOR

1 Red howler monkey
2 Peruvian spider monkey
3 Gray's bald-faced saki
4 White-fronted capuchin
5 Brown capuchin

6 Pygmy marmoset
7 Gray woolly monkey
8 Goeldi's monkey
9 Black-capped squirrel monkey
10 Emperor tamarin

11 Saddleback tamarin
12 Black-headed night monkey
13 Dusky titi
14 Brown titi

Disclaimer: Monkey silhouettes not shown to scale.

More about the Monkeys of Manú

More than 260 species of monkeys live on Earth today. About half of them live in the Americas. Scientists call them New World monkeys.

New World monkeys spend most of their time in the trees. They have small bodies, flat noses, and long, strong tails. Some can grab and hold food with their tails.

Most tropical forests are home to just a few kinds of monkeys, but Manú National Park, in southeastern Peru, is a very special place. Scientists are thrilled that 14 different monkey species live in the protected rain forest, which is a little bit smaller than the state of New Jersey. Because the monkeys of Manú have just the right combination of body features, behaviors, and lifestyles, they can all find the food and living space they need to survive. It's truly one of the most amazing communities of animals in the world.

SOUTH AMERICA

Red howler monkeys

Scientific name: *Alouatta seniculus*
Group size: 15 to 20
Diet: Mostly leaves, some nuts, fruits, seeds, flowers, and insects
Predators: Harpy eagles, jaguars
Young: One baby per year, mom provides care
Lifespan: Up to 25 years
Field note: After their midday rest, groups of howlers gather in trees and poop at the same time. Look out below!

Peruvian spider monkeys

Scientific name: *Ateles chamek*
Group size: 20 to 30, feed in subgroups of 6 to 12
Diet: Mostly fruit, some nuts, bark, leaves, insects, and bird's eggs
Predators: Jaguars
Young: One baby every 2 to 4 years, mom provides care
Lifespan: Up to 40 years
Field note: When a Peruvian spider monkey hangs from a tree by its arms, legs, and tail, it really does look like a huge spider in a web.

Gray's bald-faced sakis

Scientific name: *Pithecia irrorata*
Group size: 2 to 12
Diet: Mostly unripe fruit and seeds, some leaves, flowers, honey, insects, bird eggs, and bats
Predators: Hawks, harpy eagles, wild cats, snakes
Young: One baby every 15 months, mom provides most of care
Lifespan: Up to 30 years
Field note: If a predator gets too close, a mother saki stashes her baby in a hidden spot. Then she makes a lot of noise as she races through the forest. This usually distracts the enemy.

Brown capuchins

Scientific name: *Sapajus apella*
Group size: Up to 30, usually 8 to 15
Diet: Fruit, nuts, flowers, nectar, leaves, insects, bird eggs, baby birds, frogs, lizards, bats, and snails
Predators: Harpy eagles
Young: One baby at a time, group care
Lifespan: Up to 40 years
Field note: How do brown capuchins protect themselves from ticks and mosquitoes? By rubbing their fur with crushed millipedes and urine.

White-fronted capuchins

Scientific name: *Cebus albifrons*
Group size: 15 to 35
Diet: Mostly fruit, some nuts and insects
Predators: Harpy eagles, wild cats
Young: One baby at a time, group care
Lifespan: Up to 40 years
Field note: When white-fronted capuchins sense a predator lurking below, they spray the hungry hunter with urine.

Pygmy marmosets

Scientific name: *Cebuella pygmaea*
Group size: 2 to 9, usually 6 to 8
Diet: Mostly tree sap and insects, some fruit and nectar
Predators: Hawks, harpy eagles, wild cats, snakes
Young: Twins once or twice a year, group care
Lifespan: Up to 12 years
Field note: Pygmy marmosets are the smallest monkeys in the world. They're about the size and weight of two tennis balls.

Gray woolly monkeys

Scientific name: *Lagothrix cana*
Group size: 11 to 25
Diet: Mostly fruit, some leaves, seeds, flowers, and insects
Predators: None
Young: One baby at a time, mom provides care
Lifespan: Up to 30 years
Field note: As gray woolly monkeys search for food, they cluck like chickens and neigh like horses to stay in touch with one another.

Black-capped squirrel monkeys

Scientific name: *Saimiri boliviensis*
Group size: 10 to 50
Diet: Fruit and insects, some nectar, flowers, seeds, and leaves
Predators: Harpy eagles, wild cats, snakes
Young: One baby per year, group care by females
Lifespan: Up to 20 years
Field note: Black-capped squirrel monkeys love to play. Mama monkeys play gently with their babies. Youngsters wrestle and chase one another. Even adult males get in on the fun.

Goeldi's monkeys

Scientific name: *Callimico goeldii*
Group size: 2 to 10
Diet: Fungi, insects, fruit, spiders, scorpions, lizards, frogs
Predators: Bush dogs, wild cats, snakes, eagles, hawks
Young: One baby once or twice per year, group care
Lifespan: Up to 20 years
Field note: Goeldi's monkeys use more than 50 different calls to communicate with their friends and family.

Emperor tamarins

Scientific name: *Saguinus imperator*
Group size: 2 to 15
Diet: Fruit and flowers, some sap, insects, and frogs
Predators: Hawks, harpy eagles, wild cats, snakes
Young: Twins once a year, group care
Lifespan: Up to 20 years
Field note: Emperor tamarins were named after Emperor Wilhelm II, who ruled Germany from 1888 to 1918. Like the little monkeys, he had an impressive mustache.

Monkey sizes shown to scale.

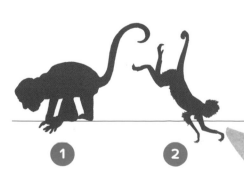

Saddleback tamarins

Scientific name: *Saguinus fuscicollis*
Group size: 4 to 20
Diet: Fruit, flowers, sap, nectar, insects
Predators: Hawks, harpy eagles, wild cats, snakes
Young: Twins once a year, group care
Lifespan: Up to 13 years
Field note: Newborn saddleback tamarin twins weigh up to 25 percent of their mother's body weight. Thank goodness her family and friends help to carry and feed the little ones.

Black-headed night monkeys

Scientific name: *Aotus nigriceps*
Group size: 2 to 5
Diet: Mostly fruit, s ome flowers, leaves, and insects
Predators: Owls, snakes, wild cats
Young: One baby per year, dad provides most of care
Lifespan: Up to 20 years
Field note: Why are black-headed night monkeys active at night? It helps them avoid most predators. It also means they don't have to compete with other monkeys for tasty fruit.

Dusky titis

Scientific name: *Callicebus moloch*
Group size: 2 to 4
Diet: Mostly fruit, some twigs, leaves, and insects
Predators: Guianan crested eagle, ornate hawk-eagle
Young: One baby per year, dad provides most of care
Lifespan: Up to 12 years
Field note: Each morning, mother and father dusky titis make loud gobbling noises. Like red howlers, they're telling other monkeys to stay out of their territory.

Brown titis

Scientific name: *Callicebus brunneus*
Group size: 2 to 4
Diet: Mostly fruit and leaves, some insects and spiders
Predators: Harpy eagle, crested eagle
Young: One baby per year, dad provides most of care
Lifespan: Unknown
Field note: Most monkeys eat just a few kinds of fruit, but brown titis feed on more than 100 different kinds of fruits and leaves.

8   9   10   11   12   13   14

Selected Sources

Attenborough, David. *The Life of Mammals.* Princeton, NJ: Princeton University Press, 2002.

Attenborough, David. *Trials of Life: A Natural History of Behavior.* New York: Little, Brown, 1990.

Cocha Cashu Biological Station. Manú National Park, Peru. cochacashu.sandiegozooglobal.org.

Discover Manú. discover-manu.org/manu.

Fleagle, John G., Charles Janson, and Kaye E. Reed, eds. *Primate Communities.* New York: Cambridge University Press, 1999.

Harvey, Paul. "Primate Adaptations." *Science,* May 18, 1984.

Marris, Emma. "One Tiny Wasp Turns a Fig Tree into a 150-Foot-High Eden." *National Geographic,* September 2016. http://news.nationalgeographic.com/2016/09/eden-in-a-fig-tree-in-the-peruvian-rainforest/.

Marris, Emma. "This Park in Peru Is Nature 'in Its Full Glory'—with Hunters." *National Geographic,* June 2016. http://www.nationalgeographic.com/magazine/2016/06/manu-peru-biodiversity-national-parks/.

Nowak, Ronald M. *Walker's Mammals of the World.* 6th ed. Baltimore, MD: Johns Hopkins University Press, 1999.

Redmond, Ian. *The Primate Family Tree: The Amazing Diversity of Our Closest Relatives.* Buffalo, NY: Firefly Books, 2008.

Stewart, Melissa. Personal observations recorded in travel journal. Tortuguero National Park, Costa Rica, 2005.

Terborgh, John. *Five New World Primates: A Study in Comparative Ecology.* Princeton, NJ: Princeton University Press, 2014.

University of Michigan Museum of Zoology. Animal Diversity Web. http://animaldiversity.org.

University of Wisconsin, Madison. National Primate Research Center's Primate Info Net. http://pin.primate.wisc.edu/.

Wright, Patricia Chapple. *High Moon over the Amazon: My Quest to Understand the Monkeys of the Night.* New York: Lantern Books, 2013.

For Further Reading

Duke, Kate. *In the Rainforest.* New York: HarperCollins, 2014.

Dunphy, Madeleine. *Here Is the Tropical Rain Forest.* Berkeley, CA: Web of Life, 2006.

Guiberson, Brenda Z. *Rain, Rain, Rain Forest.* New York: Holt, 2004.

Klepeis, Alicia. "30 Cool Things About Rain Forests." *National Geographic Kids,* September 2014.

Marris, Emma. "Peru's World Apart." *National Geographic,* student edition, June 2016.

Reid, Mary E. *Howlers and Other New World Monkeys.* Chicago: World Book, 2000.

Sayre, April Pulley. *Meet the Howlers!* Watertown, MA: Charlesbridge, 2010.

Stewart, Melissa. *No Monkeys, No Chocolate.* Watertown, MA: Charlesbridge, 2013.

Thomson, Sarah L. *Quick, Little Monkey!* Honesdale, PA: Boyds Mills Press, 2016.

To Katy Tanis, who provided key advice at just the right moment

—M. S.

For Jamie

—S. J.

BEACH LANE BOOKS • An imprint of Simon & Schuster Children's Publishing Division • 1230 Avenue of the Americas, New York, New York 10020 • Text © 2021 by Melissa Stewart • Illustrations © 2021 by Steve Jenkins • Book design by Irene Metaxatos © 2021 by Simon & Schuster, Inc. • All rights reserved, including the right of reproduction in whole or in part in any form. • BEACH LANE BOOKS is a trademark of Simon & Schuster, Inc. • For information about special discounts for bulk purchases, please contact Simon & Schuster Special Sales at 1-866-506-1949 or business@simonandschuster.com. • The Simon & Schuster Speakers Bureau can bring authors to your live event. For more information or to book an event, contact the Simon & Schuster Speakers Bureau at 1-866-248-3049 or visit our website at www.simonspeakers.com. • The text for this book was set in Proxima Nova. • The illustrations in this book are cut- and torn-paper collage. • Manufactured in China • 0421 SCP • First Edition • 10 9 8 7 6 5 4 3 2 1 • CIP data for this book is available from the Library of Congress. • ISBN 978-1-5344-6039-3 • ISBN 978-1-5344-6040-9 (eBook)